A World of Recipes

Mexico

Julie McCulloch

**Heinemann
Library**

Chicago, Illinois

© 2001 Reed Educational & Professional Publishing
Published by Heinemann Library,
an imprint of Reed Educational & Professional Publishing,
Chicago, IL

Customer Service 888-454-2279

Visit our website at www.heinemannlibrary.com

Designed by Tinstar Design
Illustrations by Nicholas Beresford-Davies
Originated by Dot Gradations
Printed by Wing King Tong in Hong Kong

05 04 03 02 01
10 9 8 7 6 5 4 3 2 1

Library of Congress Cataloging-in-Publication Data
McCulloch, Julie, 1973-

     Mexico / Julie McCulloch.
        p. cm. -- (A world of recipes)
     Includes bibliographical references and index.
     ISBN 1-58810-088-X
     1. Cookery, Mexican--Juvenile literature. 2. Cookery--Mexico--Juvenile literature. [1. Cookery, Mexican. 2. Mexico--Social life and customs.] I. Title.

TX716.M4 M393 2001
641.5972--dc21
                                          00-059743

Acknowledgments
The Publishers would like to thank the following for permission to reproduce photographs: Corbis, p. 5. All other photographs: Gareth Boden.Illustration p. 45, US Department of Agriculture/US Department of Health and Human Services.

Cover photographs reproduced with permission of Gareth Boden.

Every effort has been made to contact copyright holders of any material reproduced in this book. Any omissions will be rectified in subsequent printings if notice is given to the Publisher.

Some words in this book are in bold, **like this.** You can find out what they mean by looking in the glossary.

Contents

Key

* easy

** medium

*** difficult

Mexican Food

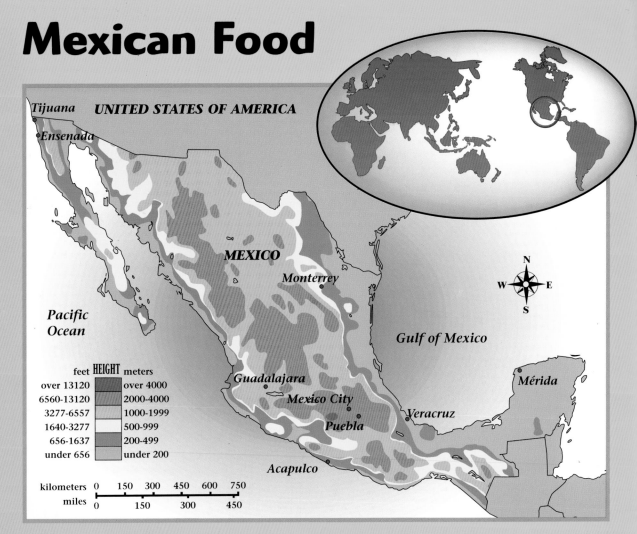

Mexico is the most southerly country in North America. Its capital, Mexico City, is one of the largest cities in the world.

Mexican people love cooking and eating. Mexican food is tasty, and there are a lot of Mexican dishes that are easy to make.

In the past

Historians believe that people have been farming in Mexico for more than 5,000 years. Early Mexicans, among them the Mayans and Aztecs, grew a wide range of crops, many of which were unknown in Europe. Their cooking ingredients included turkey, corn, tomatoes, peppers, chilies, squashes (such as pumpkin and zucchini), peanuts, avocados, guavas, chocolate, and vanilla.

In 1519, Mexico was conquered by Spain. The Spanish brought many new ingredients, such as milk, cheese, chicken, rice, wheat, cinnamon, oranges, and peaches. Today, Mexican cooking is a mixture of these different influences.

Around the country

The geography of Mexico is ideal for producing a huge range of food. The landscape varies from dry deserts in the north, to high mountains in the center of the country, to **tropical** jungles in the southeast.

These chilies growing in a Mexican field will be used in many different dishes.

Different kinds of foods are produced in different areas. In the north, cattle are raised for beef. Many different kinds of fruits and vegetables are grown in the cool mountainous areas in the middle of the country. The hotter areas in the south and around the coast produce tropical fruits such as papayas, pineapples, and coconuts. The sea provides fish and shellfish.

Mexican meals

Most people in Mexico eat their main meal at lunchtime. This meal, called *comida,* traditionally consists of three courses—an appetizer, a main course, and a dessert. *Comida* often is followed by a *siesta*—a short nap.

For breakfast, many Mexicans have coffee with milk, some sweet rolls, and maybe some yogurt. The early evening meal—*merienda*—is usually a light snack, such as cereal, sweet bread or tortillas, and hot chocolate. The day ends with *cena,* a light supper, which can be leftovers from *comida,* a potato and onion omelette, or a sandwich.

5

Ingredients

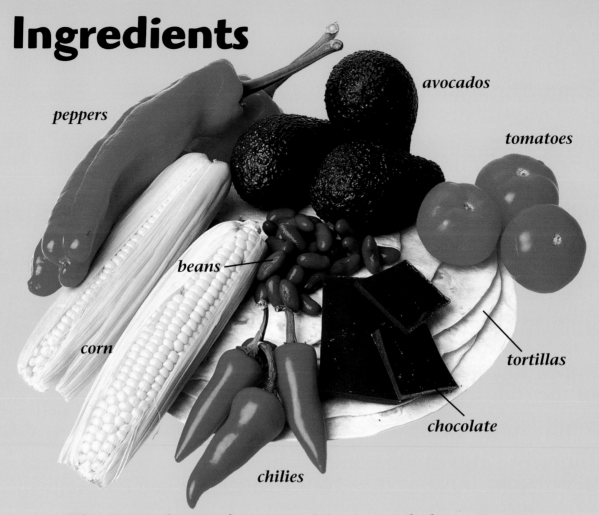

peppers

avocados

tomatoes

beans

corn

tortillas

chilies

chocolate

The ingredients for most Mexican dishes are easy to find in supermarkets and grocery stores. Here are some of the most common ones.

Avocados

Avocados originally came from Central and South America. The name avocado comes from the Mexican word *ahuacatl*. Avocados are a fruit, not a vegetable, and have a very large pit in the center.

Beans

Different beans are used in many Mexican recipes. Two of the most common types of beans are lima beans, which are used in the recipe on page 22, and kidney beans, which are used in the recipe on page 26. They are easiest to use if you buy them canned.

⚠ Chilies

Chilies are spicy peppers used in many Mexican dishes. There are hundreds of different kinds—some are mild but others are very, very hot! Fresh chilies contain an oil that can make your eyes and skin sting, so it is a good idea to use chili powder, which is made from ground-up dried chilies rather than fresh ones. If you don't like spicy food, just leave out the chili powder.

Chocolate

Chocolate has been eaten and drunk in Mexico for thousands of years. It is made from the roasted, crushed beans of the cocoa plant. In Mexico, chocolate is made into hot drinks, used in puddings, and used in sauces. Plain, dark chocolate is the best kind to use in Mexican recipes.

Corn

Corn was one of the first plants grown in Mexico, and it is used in many dishes. You can buy fresh corn on the cob, frozen corn on the cob, or as kernels separated from the cob.

Tomatoes

Tomatoes are used in many Mexican recipes. You can use either fresh or canned tomatoes in the recipes in this book.

Tortillas

Tortillas are flat circles of bread. People in Mexico eat them with many different meals. There are two different types of tortillas—wheat tortillas, which contain wheat flour, and corn tortillas, which contain flour made from ground corn. The recipe for tortillas in this book uses wheat flour.

Before You Begin

Kitchen rules

There are a few basic rules you should always follow when you cook:

- Ask an adult if you can use the kitchen.
- Some cooking processes, especially those involving hot water or oil, can be dangerous. When you see this sign, take extra care or ask an adult to help.
- Wash your hands before you begin.
- Wear an apron to protect your clothes. Tie back long hair.
- Be very careful when using sharp knives.
- Never leave pan handles sticking out—it could be dangerous if you bump into them.
- Always wear oven mitts when lifting things in and out of the oven.
- Wash fruits and vegetables before using them.

How long will it take?

Some of the recipes in this book are quick and easy. Some are more complicated and take a little longer. The strip across the top of the right-hand page of each recipe tells you how long it will take you to cook the dish from start to finish. A symbol shows you how difficult each dish is to make:

* (easy) ** (medium) or *** (difficult)

Quantities and measurements

You can see how many people each recipe will serve at the top of the right-hand page, too. Most of the recipes in this book make enough to feed two people. A few of the recipes make enough for four. You can multiply or divide the quantities if you want to cook for more or fewer people.

Ingredients for recipes can be measured in two different ways. Imperial measurements use cups, ounces, and fluid ounces. In the recipes you will see the following abbreviations:

tbsp = tablespoon   oz = ounce
tsp = teaspoon   lb = pound
ml = milliliters   cm = centimeters
g = gram

Utensils

To cook the recipes in this book, you will need these utensils, as well as kitchen essentials, such as spoons, plates, and bowls.

- baking sheet
- cutting board
- foil
- food processor or blender
- frying pan
- grater
- large, flat, ovenproof dish
- measuring cups
- potato masher
- rolling pin
- saucepan with lid
- set of measuring spoons
- sharp knife
- colander
- toothpicks

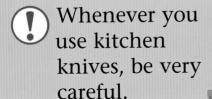

(!) Whenever you use kitchen knives, be very careful.

Tortillas

In Mexico, people eat tortillas with many different meals. Sometimes they are served as a side dish, but often they form part of the meal itself. Sometimes they are rolled around different fillings.

What you need

2/3 cup (100 g) flour (plus a few extra tbsp to sprinkle on the cutting board)
1/2 tsp salt
2 tbsp olive oil

The recipes for cheese-filled enchiladas on page 20 and fish burritos on page 30 use tortillas, so you will need to make some tortillas before cooking these dishes. You also can buy already made tortillas. Here is how to make your own.

What you do

1 Put the flour and salt into a mixing bowl. Mix in the oil with a spoon, then gradually stir in 4 tbsp warm water until the mixture starts to form a dough.

2 Sprinkle some flour onto a cutting board. **Knead** the dough until it is smooth.

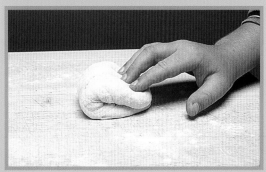

3 Divide the dough into four pieces to make four tortillas.

4 Shape one piece of dough into a ball, then flatten it.

5 Sprinkle some more flour onto the cutting board and onto a rolling pin. Roll out the dough into a circle, until it is as thin as you can make it without breaking it.

6 Heat a frying pan until it sizzles when you sprinkle a drop of water onto it. Put the tortilla into the pan.

(!) 7 Cook the tortilla for 1 minute, then turn it over and cook the other side for 30 seconds. Slide the cooked tortilla out of the pan onto a plate.

8 Repeat steps 4 through 7 with the other three pieces of dough.

STORING TORTILLAS

You can store your tortillas to use later. Put a square of wax paper between each tortilla so that the tortillas don't stick together. Allow them to **cool**, then put the stack of tortillas into a plastic bag. They will keep for several days in the refrigerator.

Guacamole

People all over Mexico eat guacamole. It can be eaten as a snack, spread on tortillas, or used as a side dish.

What you need

1 onion
handful fresh
   cilantro leaves
1/2 tsp chili powder
   (optional)
1 avocado
1 tbsp lemon juice

What you do

1 **Peel** the onion and finely **chop** half of it.

2 Finely chop the fresh cilantro.

3 In a bowl, mix together the onion, cilantro, and chili powder (if you are using it).

4 Cut the avocado in half lengthwise. Use a spoon to remove the pit.

5 Use the spoon to scoop out the flesh of the avocado. Throw the skin away.

6 Add the lemon juice to the mixture.

7 **Mash** all the ingredients together with a fork.

CILANTRO

Cilantro is an herb that comes from the leaves of the coriander plant. It is used a lot in Mexican cooking. You can usually find it in the fresh vegetable section at supermarkets. If you can't find any, try using fresh parsley leaves instead. Don't substitute dried coriander, however. This is made from the seeds, rather than the leaves, of the coriander plant and tastes completely different!

Nachos

Nachos are fried tortillas served with guacamole, cheese, and sour cream.

Frying tortillas can be dangerous, as it involves dropping tortillas into a pan of very hot oil. This recipe suggests using already made fried tortillas, which are sold in bags like chips. They are called tostadas in Mexico but often are called "tortilla chips" elsewhere.

What you need

2 servings guacamole
2 oz (50 g) cheddar cheese
1 small bag tortilla chips
1/2 cup (50 ml) sour cream

What you do

1 Make the guacamole according to the recipe on page 12.

2 **Grate** the cheese into a small bowl.

3 Put the tortilla chips into a large, flat, ovenproof dish.

4 Spoon the guacamole over the tortilla chips.

5 Spoon the sour cream over the guacamole.

6 Finally, sprinkle the grated cheese over the sour cream.

7 **Broil** the nachos for about 5 minutes, or until the sour cream is bubbling and the cheese has melted.

NACHOS WITH BEANS

A delicious variation to this recipe for nachos is to add refried beans. Put 2 tbsp of canned refried beans into a bowl and roughly **mash** them with a fork. Spread the mashed beans over the tortilla chips before adding the guacamole, sour cream, and cheese.

Corn Soup

Often, hot soup is served in the cold, mountainous regions of Mexico. Most lunches start with a bowl of soup, and many evening meals consist of soup served with a stack of tortillas. This simple corn soup is full of flavor and very **nourishing**.

If you use frozen corn, you need to **thaw** it before you use it. You can do this in two ways:

a) Take it out of the freezer at least 1 hour before you want to use it and allow it to stand; or

b) Pour hot water over the corn in a bowl, allow it to stand for 2 minutes, then carefully empty the corn into a colander to **drain**.

What you need

1 tbsp vegetable oil
1 onion
1 red pepper
1 2/3 cup (225 g) canned or frozen corn
1 **bouillon cube**
1/2 cup (125 ml) cream

What you do

1 **Peel** the onion and finely **chop** half of it.

2 Cut the red pepper in half, then scoop out the seeds. Slice half of the flesh into strips.

3 Put 1 2/3 cups of water into a saucepan and bring it to a **boil**. Drop the bouillon cube into the water and stir until it **dissolves**. Put the **stock** aside.

4 Heat the oil in a saucepan. **Fry** the chopped onion and red pepper for about 5 minutes.

5 Put the onion and pepper mixture and the corn into a blender or food processor. **Blend** until smooth.

6 Put the mixture back into the saucepan and add the stock.

7 **Simmer** the soup for about 5 minutes, until it is hot.

8 Stir in the cream. You can use the other half of the red pepper to **garnish** your soup.

COLD SOUP

This dish also can be served cold for a refreshing summer soup. Let the soup **cool**, then put it into the refrigerator for a couple of hours before serving it.

Grilled Corn on the Cob with Salsa

Ears of corn can be eaten on their own or with a sauce. This recipe shows you how to make corn on the cob with salsa, which is a spicy Mexican sauce made with tomatoes and fruit. Mexican people eat salsa with many different dishes. In Mexican restaurants, you often find a bowl of salsa on the table along with the salt and pepper.

What you need

- 1 onion
- 2 tomatoes
- 1 red pepper
- 1 slice canned or fresh pineapple
- 2 tbsp vegetable oil
- 2 ears of corn
- 1/2 tsp chili powder (if you are using it)

What you do

1 **Peel** the onion and finely **chop** half of it.

2 Chop the tomatoes into small pieces.

3 Cut the red pepper in half, then scoop out the seeds. Chop half the flesh into strips.

4 Chop the slice of pineapple into small pieces.

5 Heat 1 tbsp of the oil in a saucepan over medium heat. Add the chopped onion and the chili powder (if you are using it). **Fry** for 5 minutes, until the onion is soft.

6 Add the chopped tomatoes, red pepper, and pineapple. Turn the heat down to low and **cover** the pan. Leave the salsa to **simmer** for about 10 minutes, stirring from time to time.

7 While the salsa is cooking, brush the remaining 1 tbsp of oil onto the ears of corn.

8 Put the corn on a baking sheet under a hot **broiler** for about 10 minutes. Turn the ears often so that they cook on all sides.

9 Put the corn onto plates and spoon half of the salsa sauce onto each plate.

HOT AND SALTY

For a really quick snack, try making corn on the cob with butter and salt. Prepare the corn as described above, then spread butter on the corn while it is still hot so it melts into the corn. Sprinkle the corn with salt and eat it right away. Be careful so it doesn't burn the inside of your mouth!

Cheese-Filled Enchiladas

Enchiladas are tortillas rolled around a filling. These cheesy enchiladas are served with a hot tomato sauce.

What you need

4 tortillas (bought or homemade)

For the filling:
1/4 lb (60 g) cheddar cheese
1 cup (250 g) cottage cheese

For the tomato sauce:
1 tbsp vegetable oil
1/2 onion
1 clove garlic
1 large tomato

What you do

1 Make four tortillas using the recipe on page 10, or buy them already made.

2 **Preheat** the oven to 375°F (190°C).

3 **Peel** the onion and garlic clove and finely **chop** them.

4 Chop the tomato into small pieces.

5 Heat the oil in a frying pan over medium heat. **Fry** the chopped onion and garlic for 5 minutes, until the onion is soft but not brown.

6 Add the chopped tomato. **Cover** the pan and **simmer** the mixture for about 20 minutes, stirring from time to time.

DIFFERENT FILLINGS

You can make enchiladas with all kinds of different fillings. Here are some ideas:
- guacamole (see page 12)
- picadillo (see page 24)
- chili con carne (see page 26)

7 While the tomato sauce is simmering, **grate** the hard cheese. Mix two thirds of the cheese with all of the cottage cheese in a bowl. Keep the rest of the hard cheese for later.

8 Place 2 tbsp of the cheese mixture onto each tortilla, then roll it into a tube.

9 Put the rolled-up tortillas into an ovenproof dish coated with cooking spray.

10 Pour the tomato sauce over the rolled-up tortillas, then sprinkle the remaining hard cheese over the top.

11 Cover the dish with foil and **bake** in the oven for 30 minutes. Remove the foil and bake for another 15 minutes, until the cheese is brown and bubbling.

Bean and Potato Patties

Beans are eaten in many different ways in Mexico. You might serve these bean and potato patties with the spicy salsa recipe on page 18.

What you need

1/2 lb (250 g) potatoes
2 oz (60 g) cheddar
   cheese
1 egg
1/2 cup (125 g) canned
   lima beans
2 tbsp flour
1/2 tbsp vegetable oil

What you do

1 Carefully **peel** the potatoes using a sharp knife, then cut them into small pieces.

2 Put the potatoes into a saucepan full of water and **boil** them for about 15 minutes, until they are soft.

3 While the potatoes are boiling, **grate** the cheese into a small bowl.

4 Crack the egg into a bowl. **Beat** it with a fork or whisk until the yolk and white are mixed.

5 When the potatoes are soft, **drain** them by emptying the pan into a colander. Put the drained potatoes back into the pan.

6 Drain the lima beans by emptying the can into a colander. Put the beans into the pan with the potatoes. **Mash** the potatoes and beans together with a fork or potato masher.

7 Add the grated cheese and beaten egg to the mashed potatoes and beans. Mix everything together well.

8 Divide the mixture into four pieces and shape each piece into a flattened, round patty.

9 Sprinkle the flour onto a cutting board. Turn the patties over a couple of times on the board to coat them with flour.

! **10** Heat the oil in a frying pan over low heat. Put the patties into the pan and **fry** them gently for 10 minutes. Turn them over carefully and fry on the other side for another 10 minutes.

Picadillo

What you need

1/2 onion
1 garlic clove
1 apple
1 tbsp vegetable oil
1 large tomato
1/2 lb ground beef
1/4 tsp chili powder
   (optional)
1/2 cup (25 g) raisins
1/2 tsp cinnamon
1/2 tsp cumin

Picadillo is a main course dish made from ground beef, fruit, and spices. It is usually served with long-grain rice or tortillas.

What you do

1 **Peel** the onion and garlic clove and **chop** finely.

2 Using a sharp knife, carefully cut the apple into pieces. Throw away the core of the apple.

3 Chop the tomato into small pieces.

(!) 4 Heat the oil in a frying pan over medium heat. Add the ground beef and chopped onion and garlic.

5 **Fry** the mixture for 15 minutes, stirring from time to time, until the onion is soft and the beef is brown.

6 Add the chopped apple and tomato, chili powder (if you are using it), raisins, cinnamon, and cumin to the beef.

7 **Cover** the pan and cook the picadillo over low heat for about 15 minutes, stirring from time to time.

PICADILLO-STUFFED PEPPERS

Picadillo is sometimes served stuffed into red peppers. This looks impressive and is easy to do! Carefully cut the top off of a red pepper and scoop out the seeds. Spoon the cooked picadillo into the hollow pepper, replace the pepper's top, and **bake** in a medium oven for about 40 minutes.

Chili Con Carne

Chili con carne means "chilies with meat." Chilies are an important part of many Mexican dishes. Mexican people once believed that chilies could cure many illnesses, including toothaches and earaches. Modern science has proven that chilies do contain many **vitamins**.

What you need

1 onion
1 clove garlic
1 large tomato
1/3 cup (80 g) canned
   kidney beans
1 tbsp vegetable oil
1/2 lb (200 g) lean
   ground beef
1/2 tsp chili powder
   (optional)

What you do

1 **Preheat** the oven to 325°F (160°C).

2 **Peel** the onion and garlic clove and finely **chop** them.

3 Chop the tomato into small pieces. **Drain** the kidney beans by emptying the can into a colander.

4 Heat the oil in a frying pan over medium heat. Add the chopped onion and garlic and the ground beef.

5 **Fry** the mixture for about 15 minutes, stirring from time to time to keep it from sticking.

6 Add the chili powder (if you are using it), chopped tomatoes, and kidney beans to the pan.

7 Cook the mixture for another 5 minutes, then pour it carefully into an ovenproof dish.

8 Cover the dish and cook your chili con carne in the oven for 1 hour.

9 Spoon the cooked chili into two serving bowls. You also can serve chili with tortillas.

CHILI SIN CARNE

You can make a **vegetarian** version of this dish, called chili sin carne—chilies without meat. Just replace the ground beef with chopped vegetables, such as zucchini, mushrooms, and red peppers.

Meatballs

In Mexican cooking, ground beef is a popular filling in tacos and burritos. These meatballs are made from ground beef and make a tasty, filling main course.

What you need

1 slice stale bread
1/2 onion
1 egg
1/2 lb (200 g) ground beef
1/2 tsp dried oregano
1/2 tsp cumin
1 tbsp vegetable oil
1 vegetable **bouillon cube**

What you do

1 To make breadcrumbs, put the bread into a food processor or blender and turn it onto its highest setting for 2 minutes.

2 **Peel** the onion and finely **chop** it.

3 Crack the egg into a bowl. **Beat** it with a fork or whisk until the yolk and white are mixed.

4 Put the ground beef into a large mixing bowl. Add the breadcrumbs, chopped onion, beaten egg, oregano, and cumin.

5 Mix everything together with a spoon until it forms a smooth mixture.

6 Shape the mixture into 1 1/2-in. (3 cm) balls.

(!) **7** Heat the oil in a frying pan over medium heat. **Fry** the meatballs for about 5 minutes, turning from time to time, until they are brown.

8 While the meatballs are frying, put 1 1/3 cups (275 ml) of water into a saucepan and bring it to a **boil**. Drop in the bouillon cube and stir until it **dissolves**.

9 Pour the stock over the meatballs in the frying pan. Bring it to a boil, then **simmer** for 30 minutes.

10 Spoon the meatballs onto two plates and pour a little of the stock over them.

Fish Burritos

These are little packages of fish wrapped in tortillas. They are delicious served with the guacamole recipe on page 12. You can use fresh or frozen fish for this recipe, but make sure it is well **defrosted**.

What you need

4 tortillas
2 oz (60 g) cheddar
    cheese

For the filling

1 onion
2 fish filets (thawed
    if frozen)
1/2 tbsp vegetable oil
1/4 tsp chili powder
    (optional)
1/4 cup (50 ml) sour
    cream

What you do

1 You need four tortillas. See the recipe on page 10 to make them, or you can buy them.

2 **Preheat** the oven to 350°F (180°C).

3 **Peel** the onion and finely **chop** half of it.

4 Put the fish into a saucepan. Pour in just enough water to cover it, bring it to a **boil**, and **simmer** for 5 minutes.

(!) 5 **Drain** the water from the saucepan. Move the fish to a bowl, then **flake** it with a fork. Remove the skin and any bones.

(!) 6 Heat the oil in a frying pan over medium heat. **Fry** the onion and chili powder (if you are using it) for 5 minutes. Add this mixture to the fish.

30

7 Add the sour cream to the fish and onions and mix well.

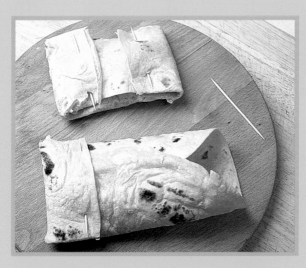

8 Put 2 spoonfuls of the fish mixture onto each tortilla. Fold the tortilla to make a square package as shown at left. Stick a toothpick through each square to keep it closed.

9 Put the burritos into an ovenproof dish coated with cooking spray.

10 **Grate** the cheese over the burritos. **Cover** the dish with foil and **bake** for 30 minutes.

11 Remove the toothpicks before serving.

Mexican Rice

This rice dish is **nourishing** enough to serve as a main course on its own. There are three different types of rice —long, medium, and short grain. This dish works best with long-grain rice.

What you need

1/2 onion
1 garlic clove
1 large tomato
1 vegetable **bouillon cube**
1 tbsp vegetable oil
2/3 cup (125) rice
1/2 tsp chili powder (optional)
1/2 cup frozen peas

What you do

1 **Peel** the onion and garlic clove and finely **chop** them.

2 Chop the tomato into small pieces.

3 Put 1 1/3 cups (275 ml) of water into a saucepan and bring it to a **boil**. Drop the bouillon cube into the water and stir until it **dissolves**. Put the stock aside.

(!) 4 Heat the oil in a saucepan over medium heat. Add the chopped onions and garlic and the rice and cook for 5 minutes, stirring all the time to keep the rice from sticking.

5 Add the chopped tomato, stock, chili powder (if you are using it), and frozen peas to the pan. Bring to a boil, then reduce the heat to low.

6 **Cover** the pan and **simmer** for about 20 minutes, stirring from time to time, until all the liquid has been soaked up.

HEALTHY EXTRAS

In some regions of Mexico, rice and beans are eaten at nearly every meal. Rice and beans are both inexpensive ingredients that are very **nourishing**. The beans provide **protein** and the rice provides **carbohydrates**.

Fruit Salad

You can serve this salad with many of the dishes in this book. It goes well with meat dishes such as picadillo and chili con carne.

What you need

1 small head of lettuce
1 carrot
1 apple
2 slices canned pineapple
1 banana
1 orange
2 tbsp lemon juice
2 tbsp vegetable oil

What you do

1 Shred the lettuce leaves and put them into a salad bowl.

2 **Peel** the carrot and **grate** it into the salad bowl.

3 **Chop** the apple into small pieces. Throw away the core of the apple. Add the apple pieces to the salad bowl.

4 **Chop** the pineapple slices into small pieces and add them to the salad bowl.

5 Peel the banana, then **slice** it into the salad bowl.

6 Peel the orange and divide it into segments. Add these to the salad bowl.

7 In a small bowl, mix the lemon juice and oil. Pour this mixture over the salad.

8 Mix, or **toss**, the salad well just before serving it.

Rice Pudding

Rice pudding is made in many different countries. This fruity Mexican version is very easy to make. This dish works best with short-grain rice.

What you need

1/3 cup (50 g) rice
1 cup (225 ml) milk
1/2 cup (100 g)
   granulated sugar
1/3 cup (40 g)
   raisins
1/2 tsp cinnamon
1/2 tbsp butter

What you do

1 Put the rice into a saucepan. Add 1/2 cup (112 ml) of water. Bring the water to a **boil**, then turn the heat down to low.

2 **Cover** the pan and **simmer** the rice for about 20 minutes, until the rice has soaked up all the water.

3 Add the milk, sugar, raisins, and cinnamon to the pan and stir everything together.

4 Cook the rice pudding over low heat, stirring all the time, until all the milk has been soaked up. This should take about 5 minutes.

5 Stir the butter into the hot rice pudding until it melts.

SOMETHING EXTRA

This rice pudding tastes really good served with fruit. Try arranging a few segments of orange or some slices of mango or papaya alongside the pudding when you serve it.

Cinnamon Oranges

Many Mexican farmers grow oranges. This refreshing dessert is very easy to make.

What you need

2 oranges
1/4 cup (25 g)
     powdered sugar
1/4 tsp ground
     cinnamon

What you do

1 **Peel** the oranges, then thinly **slice** them.

2 Place the oranges in a serving bowl.

3 Mix the sugar and the cinnamon together in a small bowl, then sprinkle this mixture over the oranges.

4 Put the cinnamon oranges in the refrigerator for at least 1 hour before serving to **chill** them.

MEXICAN DESSERTS

Sweets are very popular in Mexico. Some of the most popular desserts are made from fresh fruit, often served with spices and sugar or honey, as in this dish.

MEXICAN MARKETS

Many Mexican people buy their fruit and vegetables from street markets. Most Mexican towns have a market day, or *día del mercado*. Markets are a good place not only to shop but also to meet people.

Caramel Custard

A version of caramel custard is made in many countries around the world. In Mexico, this dish is called *flan*. It was probably brought to Mexico by the Spanish conquerors in the sixteenth century. This dish needs time to **chill** in the refrigerator, so make it several hours before you want to eat it.

What you need

2 eggs, beaten
1/2 cup (60 g) sugar
1 cup milk
a few drops of
    vanilla extract

What you do

1 **Preheat** the oven to 300°F (150°C).

2 Crack the eggs into a bowl. **Beat** them with a fork or whisk until the yolk and white are mixed.

3 Put half the sugar into a saucepan and add 1 tbsp water. Put the saucepan over low heat and stir gently until all the sugar has **dissolved**.

4 Turn up the heat and **boil** quickly, without stirring, until the mixture turns golden. Pour this syrup into one or two small custard cups.

5 Heat the milk in a saucepan over medium heat. Add the rest of the sugar and the vanilla extract. Heat for another 3 minutes, until the sugar has dissolved.

6 Stir the beaten eggs into the milk, then pour the mixture on top of the syrup at the bottom of the custard cups.

7 Put the custard cups into a large ovenproof dish. Carefully pour hot water around them until the water reaches about halfway up their sides.

8 **Cover** the ovenproof dish with foil, then put the dish in the oven and **bake** for 45 minutes.

(!) **9** Take the ovenproof dish out of the oven. Lift the custard cups out of the ovenproof dish. All the dishes will be very hot!

10 Allow the cups of custard to **cool**, then put them into the refrigerator for at least 3 hours.

11 Dip the bottom of the custard cups. into hot water to loosen the custard. Run a knife round the edges of the cups

12 Quickly turn the custard out onto a plate before serving.

Mexican Hot Chocolate

Chocolate, cinnamon, and vanilla are classic Mexican flavors. In fact, Mexican chocolate bars often have cinnamon and vanilla added to them.

What you need

- 1/2 cup (125 g) dark chocolate, broken into chunks
- 2 cups (500 ml) milk
- 1/2 tsp ground cinnamon
- a few drops of vanilla extract

What you do

1 Break the chocolate into pieces. Put them into a nonmetallic, microwavable bowl.

2 Place the bowl in the microwave and cook on medium (50 percent) power for 1 minute, stirring every 20 seconds until the chocolate is completely melted.

3 Warm the milk in a small saucepan. Slowly stir half the milk into the melted chocolate. Pour the chocolate and milk mixture back into the saucepan with the rest of the milk.

4 Stir in the cinnamon and vanilla extract. Heat for a few more minutes.

5 Pour the hot chocolate into two cups.

COLD CHOCOLATE

You also can use this recipe to make a cold chocolate drink. Allow the hot chocolate to **cool**, then whisk it with a fork or whisk before pouring it into cups.

BREAKFAST BREAD

Hot chocolate is sometimes served with *pan de yema,* a type of bread cooked in egg yolks, which is similar to French toast. The bread is dipped into the hot chocolate.

More Books

Cookbooks

Coronado, Rosa. *Cooking the Mexican Way.* Minneapolis, Minn.: Lerner Publications, 1989.

England, Tamara. *Josefina's Cook Book: A Peek at Dining in the Past with Meals You Can Cook Today.* Madison, Wis.: Pleasant Company, Inc., 1998.

Illsley, Linda. *A Taste of Mexico.* Austin, Tex.: Raintree Steck-Vaughn, 1994.

Books About Mexico

Alcraft, Rob, and Sean Sprague. *Mexico.* Chicago, Ill.: Heinemann Library, 1997.

Gresko, Marcia S. *Letters Home from Mexico.* Woodbridge, Conn.: Blackbirch Press, 1999.

Comparing Weights and Measures

3 teaspoons = 1 tablespoon	1 tablespoon = 1/2 fluid ounce	1 teaspoon = 5 milliliters
4 tablespoons = 1/4 cup	1 cup = 8 fluid ounces	1 tablespoon = 15 milliliters
5 1/3 tablespoons = 1/3 cup	1 cup = 1/2 pint	1 cup = 240 milliliters
8 tablespoons = 1/2 cup	2 cups = 1 pint	1 quart = 1 liter
10 2/3 tablespoons = 2/3 cup	4 cups = 1 quart	1 ounce = 28 grams
12 tablespoons = 3/4 cup	2 pints = 1 quart	1 pound = 454 grams
16 tablespoons = 1 cup	4 quarts = 1 gallon	

Healthy Eating

This diagram shows which foods you should eat to stay healthy. You should eat 6–11 servings a day of foods from the bottom of the pyramid. Eat 2–4 servings of fruits and 3–5 servings of vegetables a day. You should also eat 2–3 servings from the milk group and 2–3 servings from the meat group. Eat only a few of the foods from the top of the pyramid.

Mexican cooking uses many ingredients from the bottom of the pyramid, such as rice and tortillas. Mexican cooking also includes many fresh fruits and vegetables. Beans, meat, fish, and cheese are popular ingredients in Mexican cooking, too.

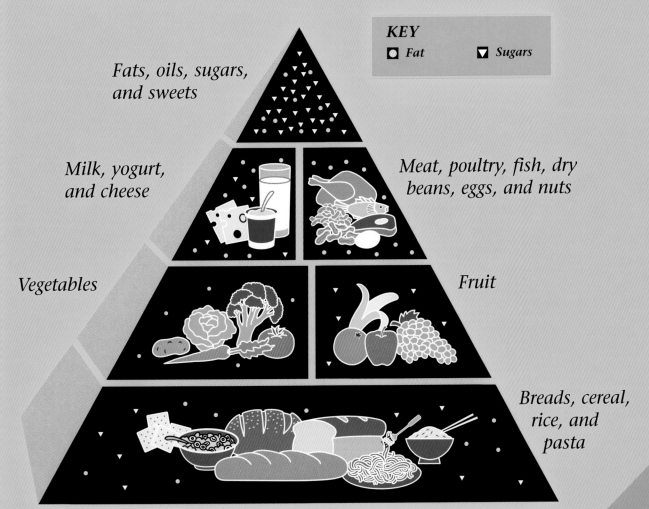

Fats, oils, sugars, and sweets

KEY
◻ *Fat*   ▽ *Sugars*

Milk, yogurt, and cheese

Meat, poultry, fish, dry beans, eggs, and nuts

Vegetables

Fruit

Breads, cereal, rice, and pasta

Glossary

bake to cook something in the oven

beat to mix something together strongly, for example egg yolks and whites

blend to mix ingredients together in a blender or food processor

boil to cook a liquid on the stovetop until it bubbles and steams strongly

broil to cook something over or under an open flame

carbohydrate food that contains sugar and starch, such as potatoes, and that gives us energy

chill to put a dish in the refrigerator for several hours before serving

chop to cut something into small pieces with a knife

cool to allow hot food to become cold, especially before putting it into a refrigerator

cover to put a lid on a pan or foil over a dish

defrost to allow something that is frozen to reach room temperature

dissolve to stir something, such as sugar, until it disappears into a liquid

drain to remove liquid from a pan or can of food

flake to break something, for example a piece of fish, into small pieces, often with a fork

fry to cook something by placing it in hot oil or fat

garnish to decorate using food

grate to shred something by rubbing it back and forth over a utensil that has a rough surface

knead to mix ingredients into a smooth dough

mash to crush something until it is soft and pulpy

nourishing food that is good for our bodies and our health

peel to remove the skin of a fruit or vegetable

preheat to turn on the oven in advance, so that it is hot when you are ready to use it

protein body-building material found in some foods, such as beans, eggs, and meat

simmer to cook a liquid on the stovetop just under a boil

slice to cut something into thin, flat pieces

thaw to allow something that has been frozen to come to room temperature

toss to mix ingredients together roughly, as in a salad

tropical hot, wet climate

vegetarian diet that usually does not include meat or fish, and that sometimes does not include eggs or dairy products; person who follows such a diet

vitamins substances our bodies get from food to stay healthy

Index